For Sally, Sadie and Eve

FOREWORD

It is both a pleasure and a privilege to be invited to say a few words of introduction to *The Iron Harvest*, the first full collection of poems by my friend Mick Jenkinson. W. H. Auden famously said that the ambition of most poets is to be both 'valued locally and prized elsewhere' – a statement that applies particularly to Mick who, while writing out of the landscape of his native South Yorkshire, finds a universality that appeals to those who live outside the region. In this respect, *The Iron Harvest* of the title resonates deeply as both a comment on the physical struggle to bring things to the surface but also to the sense of the poems themselves being part of that process.

There is something characteristically uncompromising in this, drawing attention as it does to the historical struggles that took place in this region – and to the process by which the individual poems in the collection were gathered together and harvested into something considered and, ultimately, moving. Jenkinson's deep affinity with the land and the people who live there is the continuum that threads these poems together, taking love poems, poems of protest and cultural change, and poems from both autobiographical and collective memory, and arranging them into a sequence which gives them added strength and resonance.

Those familiar with Mick Jenkinson's work will find much here that connects to his previous writing. In both *A Tale to Tell* (Glass Head Press, 2017) and *When the Water's Rise* (Calder Valley Poetry, 2019) he mapped out a poetic territory which he continues to expand and explore in *The Iron Harvest,* in which the opening poem, *The River* is a hymn to the Don which flows through the City of Doncaster and the surrounding landscape. It ends with a sense of recognition, a feeling of inevitability, and acts as a perfect introduction to the poems that are to come:

> *And this river*
>
> *that's always run*
>
> *through everything I've ever done*
>
> *flows on beside me*

While landscape provides the common ground for these poems, they deal also with the people who inhabit it, whether they be our prehistoric ancestors arriving into the valley for the first time and deciding to settle there, or present-day urban-dwellers facing the challenges of twenty-first century living. There is a sharp and uncompromising political consciousness at work throughout, surfacing from the poems about landscape and growing environmental concerns. *When the Waters Rise*, for instance, imagines the very real threat of towns, cities, and communities being islanded and inundated by the effects of global warming. It is one of the best poems in a collection that shifts effortlessly across its whole range of subjects, facilitated by Jenkinson's control of language and poetic form.

Here too we find variety as well as depth. Jenkinson has a confident way with traditional forms – but he never uses them in order for them to draw attention to themselves; rather one feels that the forms themselves are inseparable from the meaning; that to move them into a different form would change the whole premise of the poem. This formal control is what gives him the ability to write with such confidence. While exhibiting an interest in, and control of formal aspects, Mick Jenkinson also experiments with freer forms. The result here is to produce a hesitancy, a sense of an intelligence working its way tentatively through the intricacy of the poem yet never suggesting that what the reader is encountering is anything other than accessible and engaging. His voice is distinctive and his poetic identity easily recognisable.

While there are many individual poems that stand out, one of the finest is *Past Brodsworth* which acts as an effective anchor for the whole book. As with many of the best poems in *The Iron Harvest* it is located in the past, and in this instance the personal past of the poet as well as the historical past of the landscape he remembers himself in as a child. Jenkinson has captured a very moving moment here, one in which his grandmother shows him the Don Valley as if she is passing the whole of its provenance onto him. He becomes something of a custodian of the place, honour bound to perpetuate its stories and connections in his life and work. Encouraging him to look deeply, with his inner eye, she tells him

> *you will see traces and remains of what made us*
>
> *in the light down the valley, in the air above the fields*
>
> *and in the prints of your shoes.*

It is a tender, inexplicable moment, given expression by this fine poet. Other such moments occur throughout this collection.

To finish on a personal note, Mick Jenkinson has been my song writing partner for almost a decade now, providing music for my lyrics. His ability to understand the nuances of language and find a musical equivalent is remarkable and working with him in collaboration has been one of highlights of my life as a poet. I'm sure Mick's profound gift informs the musicality of these poems where the sound they make is as important as the meaning they convey. Much like Edward Thomas (a poet he admires) the sound and sense are intrinsically connected at a very deep level and expressed in a language which is alert to the natural rhythms of the speaking voice. Most importantly of all, Mick Jenkinson understands his audience and writes both for us and with us finding in the landscape of his birth what Shakespeare's would have called 'a local habitation and a name'.

Dr Ian Parks

2024

Contents

This River	9
Oysters	10
Kindling	11
The Land Rises	12
Pareidolia	13
Enduring Marks	14
Halki	15
The Lighthouse	16
Falling in Love	17
The Old Year	18
The Story	20
The Horologist	21
The Porch	23
Drinking Your Fill	24
A Tale to Tell	25
We Will March Today	27
What Are We Expected to Do?	28
Broken	29
The Hurt	30
Leaves Are Falling	31
Herald	32
Hometown	33
This Is Our Time	34
The Wrong Man	35
Damage	36
Rannoch	38
Craig Varr	39
A Spoonful of Honey in a Barrel of Tar	41
Vergissmeinnicht	42
Seeds	43
Belonging	44

Apparition	45
Sweep the Floor	46
Last Tram to Middlewood	48
Heading for the Sea	49
Unbroken	50
Log Store	51
Blue to Black	52
Half Past Autumn	53
Iron Harvest	54
Transgression	55
You Leave	56
Walking	57
Potteric Carr	59
Beyond the Salutation	60
Three Engine Blocks	61
Woodfield Road	62
Water in the Well	63
When the Waters Rise	64
Is This What Leaving Feels Like?	66
Renewal	67
Departure	68
Beyond the Espaliered Pear Tree	69
Tom's Territory	70
Encounter	71
Crossroads	73
Termination	74
Wide Open	75
Thin Skin	76
One Thing More	78
Past Brodsworth	79
Notes and Acknowledgements	81

This River

My God will probably reside
somewhere along,
somewhere beside this river.
My God will probably reside
beside the River Don –
not in some sleepy white
Andalucian hilltop aldea,
nor in the hazy light
of a tropical island shore,

but down, deep down
here in the Don Gorge
where scintillae through high trees
turn sceptics to devotees –
flashing white
on dolomite.

And this river
that's always run
through everything I've ever done
flows on beside me.

Oysters

Who's never felt this way,
with dreams of the quixotic –
yearning to be provocative,
bizarre, sexy, exotic?

I taste of where I'm from –
my brackish territory:
so take me with a shot of stout
or Hemingway Daiquiri,

then feel me in your mouth,
an extraordinary thing.
I'm salty, briny, fishy-fresh,
I'll make your spirit sing.

Take me au naturel,
with gimlet or dirty martini,
swallow slowly to release
the sweetness, the umami.

Savour me with absinthe,
sip me with champagne,
devour me like your senses
will never soar this way again.

Kindling

Already the light is leaving.
See the afternoon pack its bags with a steady shrug,
smelling of a season still a month away.

We are gathering up kindling,
telling each other survival stories,
the need for bodily warmth –
not daring to move closer in these singular times.

We all end up sometimes praying,
most more out of fear than faith,
helpless desperation –
exasperation that all else has failed.

The Land Rises

There's a sharp spring breeze that stings
your early morning cheeks.
Before the walkers and the cyclists
come, you could be anywhere.

See how the land here rises
and the path forks as we climb.
Taking one; we'll no doubt choose
the other, should we come again.

The dogs tear through the spinneys
that have waited forty years
and counting, to begin to tell
their stories of renewal.

The land rises more slowly,
flattens out to grass and shrub,
and you can see from here the wheel
in stone, down by the edge of town.

This month, it seems it's barely stopped –
lashing, bucketing, unforgiving –
leaving black stained puddles where
the land still leeches memories.

Pareidolia

You wouldn't take it lightly,
would you –
those stories stencilled up there
which you're so eager to read?

There's more to be discovered
than you've seen or imagined
in the sparkling silver,
the brooding black –
binding up your dreams
in their mercurial reality.

You'd be a fool
to bet against them,
those shapes that make sense,
shift, and then don't.

Enduring Marks

I can't recall what led up to that kiss
or why I'd never lost hold of the spark
Who would believe that it should be like this?

The mattresses, the music, could I miss
those eyes that cut across the raucous talk?
I can't recall what led up to that kiss

The frenzy faded; what remained was us
The world has granted us this holy dark
Who would believe that it should be like this?

Fumbling hands that learned what passion is
Exhilarated by your scent and silk
I can't recall what led up to that kiss

Down all the years, betrayed by distances –
news of the morning that you never woke
Who would believe that it should be like this?

Maybe life's best defined by absences –
brief moments etched the most enduring marks
I can't recall what led up to that kiss
Who would believe that it should be like this?

Halki

From this terrace, right now,
you can see everything you'll ever need to see.
Across the bay the lights of the harbour lie quiet
and still in this warm, reassuring night.
Constellations wider, deeper, clearer,
in a blue-black sky that wraps us tight.

From this terrace, right now,
you can feel the lapping
of the waves across millennia.
Pelasgi, Kares, Durians, and Phoenicians
through to Turk, Italian and Greek
have all taken shelter here.

Then there's you
with your golden hair tumbling as you come,
pouring Metaxa and drawing your chair close,
taking my arm to share the vigil.
I was reading Cavafy before you insisted
we turn off the terrace lights:
Try, if possible, not to waste your life
although it might not work out as you planned.

The Lighthouse

The lighthouse spins its ray
through cooling evening air
out across the bay.

At closing of the day
she walked with me out here –
the lighthouse spins its ray.

I watched the precious way
she smiled. She shook her hair
out across the bay.

All I can do is say
My time I'll gladly share.
The lighthouse spins its ray.

Knowing she'd never stay
was more than I could bear.
Out across the bay

she said *it's all ok*.
I stand alone and stare.
The lighthouse spins its ray
out across the bay.

Falling in Love

She said - *I don't feel right, I feel kind of strange*
I said - *I've got to tell you I've been feeling the same*
She said - *I can't eat; I go weak at the knees*
I said - *those things, they've been happening to me*
Now I'm in no shape to tell you what's real and what's not
I'm just making a guess at what it is that we've got
It feels like falling in love

I've seen people's faces, I've heard what they say
I never could work out what made them that way
I've had it described to me so many times
I'm not complaining, I really don't mind
I've seen it in films, read about it in books
It gets me confused, but unless I've mistook
It feels like falling in love

Whatever it is, it's keeping me awake
In the day I'm distracted, my bones start to ache
She said - *well, you must have caught it from me*
I said - *the way it looks, it seems a certainty*
The only solution is a spell of quarantine
We could get locked up together till we find out what it means
It feels like falling in love

The Old Year

The satisfying crunch
of the grass underfoot
and branches newly jewelled
in first light.

Watery sun bleeding
along the horizon,
distant mists dispersing
as it climbs.

Witnessing the garden
before the kettle boils;
nothing much to report
of the old year.

Scattered splash of yellow
and rust-red clinging on
with tendrils seeking still
to persevere.

These last few nasturtiums
whose heads wearily droop,
till conquered by the frost
they'll finally fall.

A pause along the path
to gaze up at the ash
as if the tree held lessons
you could learn.

The earth is sleeping now,
you can hear the soil sigh,
so listen for what truth
you might discern.

The Story

Life had been a succession of anti-climaxes,
dead-ends, seclusion, longing,
scraping by in a small town below stone skies,
seemingly empty trains rattling past,
unsent letters propped on the dresser.

There lay the story close to his heart,
one as compromised as life and death –
it wasn't the story he'd set out to tell,
nor the one the world wanted to hear,
but it was the story, nonetheless.

The Horologist

I'll tell you about time
You see enough, you come to understand
how shallow the conceit
that one might influence the falling sand

The tiresome tick and tock
my patience never tested so before
The plague's relentless mock
beat us till we in blind obeisance swore

I need to clean my hands
this work requires a sterile atmosphere
Should you wish to observe
then do the same before you enter here

Bring me your broken clock
chronometer or clepsydra to mend
This is my element
a steady eye and yet more steady hand

I'll show to you whole worlds
within the shifting gears of this chablon
but out beyond these walls
who can be sure that life and love go on?

And though time finds its voice
from pockets, mantle pieces and bell towers
these clocks can only serve –
each timepiece striking off life's hollow hours

When all of this is done
would you meet me by the meridian?
We'll take a quiet turn
I'll tell you of the great John Harrison

The Porch

You said a painted shack was good enough;
a little place that overlooks the sea
and maybe with a little greenery,
a piece of dirt where we could plant some stuff.

It was one of those late-night conversations
when things you dare not say get somehow said,
became more intimate than we intended,
the evening's drinking lowering inhibitions.

And did I really say I'd held a torch
and always willed an evening such as this?
And if, or not, this night ends with a kiss,
one day we'll sit together on that porch.

Drinking Your Fill

My heart's a nest of ants –
it won't be still
it won't ever be still

You come, all dusk and blush –
your elusive skill
your elusive, empyrean skill

With quiet confidence –
exerting your will
effortlessly exerting your will

You never dealt in half measures –
drinking your fill
insatiably drinking your fill

I'm emptied out, ecstatic –
time stands still
this wrung-out time stands still

A Tale to Tell

Huddled in the courtyard,
struggling to recall.
Telling each other half-stories
of the time before the fall.

Sometimes a snatch of a refrain,
a fragment of a verse,
a part-remembered blessing
or the couplet of a curse.

Has anyone a tale to tell of the time before the sky fell?
Who will learn our new song and pass it on?

When the daylight breaks,
the purpose has been served;
it can never be taken from us
once this moment is preserved.

Nights might be dark and deep,
they may still be cold and long,
but they have lost their terror for us
now we have and hold this song.

Has anyone a tale to tell of the time before the sky fell?
Who will learn our new song and pass it on?

Words will stretch for meaning,
melody grasp at hope;

the disaffected and dislocated
will find surprising ways to cope.

There will be fresh indignities
and passing times of joy;
astonishing ways for a girl to gaze
into the eyes of a boy.

Has anyone a tale to tell of the time before the sky fell?
Who will learn our new song and pass it on?

We Will March Today

We will march today for hope and equality.
We will march today as if we can change the world
with our simple badges, placards, and banners unfurled –
condemned for our innocence of stratagems and polity.

We will march today against false truths and lies.
We will march today against the sickness that is brewing.
We will not recognise limits to what we are doing
when we are condemned and demonised.

We will march today to be visible.
We will march today as we should have done before.
We failed to read the signs, and what can't be ignored
will be condemned as little more than risible.

We will march today in sedition.
We will march today with unlikely bedfellows;
a motley collection under a flag of rainbows
who will be condemned as the wrong sort of opposition.

We will march today against the inevitability.
We will march today as we no longer know our place.
We will come together; organise; resist; embrace
and be condemned for our manifest futility.

We will march today in anger and in sorrow.
We will march today against those who declare it pointless.
We will seek answers we do not yet possess.
We will be condemned; and we will march tomorrow.

What Are We Expected to Do?

The landing is strewn with legend and fable;
revision aids and boy-band CD's.
We look at each other across the kitchen table –
what are we expected to do with these?

Two spare bedrooms no one ever stays in;
empty chairs at the evening meal;
a garden of toys that nobody plays in –
what are we expected to know and feel?

Broken

On the tip of her tongue
as with so many others;
the neighbours we spoke of
as sisters and brothers –
who would take
something so precious and break it?

The flowers that bloomed
from seeds we had planted;
is this not what we
worked for and wanted –
who would see
something that lovely and break it?

Cicadas still sing
on Mediterranean shores
of once-cherished things
we will do no more –
who can hear
a song such as this and break it?

Illusionist in the wings, he waits for his cue;
a woman in a box – he'll saw her in two,
but the curtain comes down,
the crowd strangely stilled,
with no one sure whether
she really was killed –
who could believe
such a spell could ever be unbroken?

The Hurt

Did you see enchantment in her eyes?
They flashed like the clash of swords.

Your self-control, inconstant as ice
in this flame you are drawn towards.

She sets your senses on fire,
she brings out your mad desires,

she shows you heaven with your face in the dirt,
for when she comes, she brings the hurt.

Shadows of old ghosts, they warn you
with hollow eyes and lips so blue.

She is a stranger to you
and she's all you ever knew.

She is *la belle dame sans merci,*
she is life and death, you'll see –

the feast is set, but there'll be no dessert,
for when she comes, she brings the hurt.

Leaves Are Falling

After such a year
how much further
can the world fall
before it begins
to heal?

Amid the sadness
where's the incantation
to be found
to awaken what's been
asleep too long?

Among dead ashes
what will it take
to blow those
sparks of hope
into a flame?

Leaves are falling
and it's always an end
or a beginning
of something.

Herald

I'm waiting, watching,
willing the daybreak
to deliver respite
from the dread of night.

The weak sun
divides a black cloud,
tipping over
this crater's edge,

and is tinted by torn flesh,
filtered through abandoned armaments –
the heartless herald of each new day.

Hometown

I always end up on my highest horse
when sensing that my town is being defamed.
I summon quiet anger and resource,
refute the slanderous things that others claim.
This town's been ravaged, battered, beaten down;
its riches plundered and its glory days
dismissed to history; left without renown,
which cynicism so glibly betrays.
But this town harbours riches in great store:
a spirit that refuses to be cowed,
a story of survival and much more,
a people not too humble, nor too proud.
This is where we measure our own worth:
there's beauty in these streets and in this earth.

This Is Our Time

Watching as the school bus goes by,
we jangle change in trouser pockets,
spend the fare on 4-a-penny Black Jacks
from the machine behind the Esso station.

Running through the graveyard of St Edmunds
and past the wooden scout hut at the back,
with nettles stinging our short trousered legs
and blazers snagged on tangles of brambles,

not pausing where the track is overgrown,
to long-abandoned cottages
whose ruins become our own secret land,
with no surveillance from the grown-up world.

The rope swing takes us from the rowan tree
across the oily dyke, to where
a sign high on the fence says *Razor Wire*
Do not climb and do not enter here.

But we'll come here again and again.
This is our time, and this is our domain;
buried treasure, hidden jewels,
where we and only we will make the rules.

In this place you could lose yourself forever.
Time has no importance when
you're playing out these strategies and battles,
but we'll really catch it if we're late for tea.

The Wrong Man

I know that you've won,
but I still can't concede;
I don't have the wants,
but I do have the needs.
I feel all the failings
like hunger and greed;
unsavoury senses
I still have to feed.

If you're looking for passion,
there's a ready supply;
if you're expecting compassion,
don't look too close in my eye.
I don't mind you talking,
it's just what you say –
it sticks in my ears
and it won't go away.

Remorse and contrition,
I can keep them at bay;
it's a fateful condition,
it might haunt me one day.
There are things that we're saying
I know I'll regret,
and things that we've done
I'm trying hard to forget.

You've got the wrong man –
don't you understand?

Damage

I'm overcome by roses and by limes –
my first intoxication by perfume –
it comes to me at most peculiar times.

The shimmer of the air inside this room
like rain that stipples the surface of the sea
or dreams that are waiting to resume –

Why are you here? I'm not even asleep.
Why did you have to come round here tonight?
The past is gone, the secret's mine to keep.

But she said *There are wrongs you need to right*
and we have business that's still incomplete.
You should have learned by now to be contrite.

The memories that we share are bittersweet;
the endurance of a glance or of a touch,
but don't take consolation from conceit.

The harm you did that fateful night was such
you pulled away my thread of self-esteem
and left me feeling I was not worth much.

I said *Things are not always as they seem.*
I feel as if I'm fighting the same wars;
will you not bring some stillness to my dream?

She said *You never took the time to pause;*
consider asking what it is I need
or recognise the hurt that you could cause.

If I could have that time again, I'd heed
those words; I'd try to make amends and soothe
the pain; make recompense for those misdeeds,

but then, we all have our own take on truth
to reach accommodation with our crimes:
the casual indifference of youth.

I'm overcome by roses and by limes –
my first intoxication by perfume –
it comes to me at most peculiar times.

Rannoch

The mist parts,
I look over the water to the southern shore.
I am reminded why I am drawn back
to this light
that renders everything more

alive, more sensual.
Summer green slipping to autumn gold
that proclaims why I come here
to this light;
shades multiplied a hundredfold.

When the sun
tears the sky, slams its light against the lake,
the spirit in me is lifted up
to this light
as a thousand stars explode in its wake.

Craig Varr

I neglected to pack my map;
the thought hangs around, nagging at me.
It can't detract
from the beauty of this crag –
bracken and autumn beech trees
on its southern slope.

The path is not badly marked;
steep in places, but solid underfoot
despite recent rains,
whose issue has made magnificent torrents
from last week's meagre cascades
over polished gritstone.

An impressive old hazel coppice,
big stepping stones across a boggy stretch,
then the path rises
by a tumbledown stone wall
in the shadow of venerable oaks,
marking the old drovers' road.

I rest at the fountainhead,
stooping with a cupped hand in a ritual nod
to this ancient water source,
and turning to breathe the air,
take in the glory of
those views across the water.

The plan was to climb and climb
till that rocky outcrop was my window
on the world, but I see every peak
has a heavy halo of dripping mist
that is beginning to roll
in this brooding place of storms.

A Spoonful of Honey in a Barrel of Tar

A spoonful of honey in a barrel of tar.
What did you expect from this life –
champagne wishes and caviar?

They say you're no better than you are,
gratuitously twisting the knife –
a spoonful of honey in a barrel of tar.

Striving to make things better than par,
but in the end, all your dreams come to strife;
champagne wishes and caviar.

A bloke says to me, late night at the bar:
Negativity these days is rife –
a spoonful of honey in a barrel of tar.

I'll beat out this tune on an old guitar,
for love of good friends, my children and wife.
Champagne wishes and caviar?

Make a wish on a shooting star;
it's the here and now, not the afterlife:
a spoonful of honey in a barrel of tar.
Champagne wishes and caviar.

Vergissmeinnicht

Your bags are packed, the atmosphere stands taut;
today you will resume your wandering.
Above our constant overshadowing
the air turns heavy, and the clouds grow swart.

This afternoon drifts into somnolence
as sluggish shadows shift across the grass.
There's no sweet reverie in this impasse;
could we be both lovers and combatants?

There's damage often wrought by idleness,
though when we loved, we never did so lightly,
but even days that beckon us so brightly
can soon be squandered by our carelessness.

A chill wind stirs, a shudder in the tree;
I take your hand, and you return my gaze.
We salvage harmony from the malaise,
won't part dishonoured by the hurt that we

no longer have the stomach to inflict.
Your train is due, I hear its distant whistle.
You joke, *your favourite flower is the thistle*,
while I say *yours will be vergissmeinnicht.*

Seeds

Resist the temptation to tally tasks
you didn't get to do;
this no day for self-recrimination,
but to be looking out
on this dissolute late summer garden,
its raggedy magnificence.

There's nothing here
that will not be enhanced
by idle contemplation,
and neither would the world
be much improved
by some remorseful mood.

A day's vindication. If you believe
it rests in moments
of incidental wonder,
then watch with me a while
as these weeds
gleefully cast down seeds.

Belonging

They say that exile clarifies things – who can tell?
To ask 'county or country' is to miss the point;
it's not something that's easy to articulate
and neither is it a matter of volition.
We stop for a sandwich in the leeward shelter
of a drystone wall on a high Pennine ridge.
A profound, wordless conversation is unfolding –
I could be with my father, or with my own daughter.

The sky is stoic; by turns threatening and comforting.
We look down on the cities while we yearn for the moors –

we carry this with us wherever, forever.

Apparition

I lay my eyes on you
to observe how you hold your pen;
wait for you to turn
and then
I can drink your gaze;
feeling more like myself than ever before.

I lay my eyes on you;
wait to see what you eat when you rise;
how you face each new day
and then
it leaves me amazed;
feeling more like myself than ever before.

I lay my eyes on you
to discover what the books are you read;
measure your needs and desires
and then
I feel my spirit blaze;
feeling more like myself than ever before.

I lay my eyes on you,
you, with your flowers and perfumes.
I rub ash into my skin
and then
it might have been seconds, might have been days;
feeling more like myself than ever before.

Sweep the Floor

If we had never met
you could not leave me with
no prospect of a fond farewell
but what then would I be
and how would I recall
the time we didn't get to fill?

I first would sweep the floor
ensure the rubbish bins
were emptied and the worktops clean
Each trace would be erased
of all the wreckage and
the ruins of what might have been

The cupboards rearranged
I'd throw away the stuff
for which I'd have no further use
stuff we might have shared –
long past its useful life –
that sought exactly this excuse

Not needing company
and happy in my skin
I'd then discover small routines
No need for much at all –
keep my focus sharp
to hold at bay the unforeseen

I'd not be maudlin, but
absorbed in what it takes
to live a solitary life
not to get side-tracked
nor spare you miles of thoughts
of emptiness and pain and loss

Last Tram to Middlewood

Another business meeting never reaching resolution,
he could not find the courage to curtail.
He grabs his coat and hat and takes the stairs down from the office
to see his tram slide through the evening veil.

He looks round for a phone box as he fumbles for loose change,
he'd promised her he'd make this rendezvous.
His fingers drag the dial around, he's praying that she'll answer,
they'd try one final time to talk it through.

He hears the clicking of the line, he stutters his excuses,
they'd taken this route many times before.
He grips the cold receiver as he's deafened by the silence,
barely notices the line go dead once more.

Last tram to Middlewood, as grey fades into black;
his last chance disappearing down the track.

Heading for the Sea

The evening light is turning,
won't you step outside your door?
There's an orange sunset burning
like you've never seen before.

We'll walk down to the bridge
to where the rushing waters flow
down from the mountains to the ocean
over rocks forever more.

A path leads from this road
where, if you match me stride for stride
we'll talk, and share our thoughts and dreams
before the ebbing tide.

While on the distant shores of Skye,
just leaving from the quay,
a blue and yellow painted boat
is heading for the sea.

Unbroken

It was always too delicate by half,
conjuring memories of Saturdays –
armchair afternoons, racing on TV,
cradled safe in the crook of your huge arm;
the willow pattern mug always steaming.

In my usual rush to get home from work,
placed the half-drunk cuppa on the van roof,
loaded up, drove away without thinking.

Log Store

The chainsaw you returned to me
and nattered on interminably
on technicalities
of tree felling.

You'd kept the thing for far too long –
my winter store of firewood gone
and no apologies
were forthcoming.

You said you had sharpened the chain
and that would help ease the back pain
linked inextricably
to log sawing.

That may or may not have been sincere –
you died in your sleep that same year –
it never was, really,
worth pursuing.

You'd clearly run it without oil
and from that time would always fail
to fire – tellingly,
its undoing.

Blue to Black

I watch a cloud, like ice cream, melt;
horizon turns from blue to black.
Captain says fasten your safety belt.

You play the hand that you've been dealt
or fold it back into the pack.
I watch a cloud, like ice cream, melt.

Wind might howl, rain might pelt;
I pray the courage that I lack.
Captain says fasten your safety belt.

We're Anglo Saxon, Norman, Celt,
and more exotic DNA too, Jack.
I watch a cloud, like ice cream, melt.

The warning signs were badly spelt;
it seems the whole world's out of whack.
Captain says fasten your safety belt.

It's hard to express how I felt;
all I can do to keep on track.
I watch a cloud, like ice cream, melt.
Captain says fasten your safety belt.

Half Past Autumn

Half past autumn, the pumpkin, the smoke,
and morning mist drops heavy dew.
Trees sag, as if those few final leaves
hold the weight of the world.

Last of the swallows upped and gone,
thoughts turn to comfort, food, warmth;
gathering together for talks by the fire,
feeling the pull of home.

Time to be foraging for winter store,
for plots, plans and sustenance.
Treasure now these frost-hardy brassicas –
munitions against melancholy.

This is how your heart learns to survive
as the world gets older and harder:
not quite winter, but a premonition –
bring on the snow angels.

Iron Harvest

This February it was courage
that the plough turned from the soil –
its form, a rusted, twisted
corrupted barbed wire coil –
a cage for vacant shadows
to play their torment and turmoil.

Last early spring was outrage
that our tilling tools revealed –
a four-foot pock-marked shell case
hauled up from the field
shouting out *injustice*
when will you be healed?

So it is with this season's turn,
each year we scour and scourge
revenant recollections,
desperate to emerge:
more twisted steel ordnance
thrown to the field's verge.

Next year or soon enough
so the stories abound,
when we newly split the earth
as the season comes around,
it will be answers, explanations,
we haul from the sickened ground.
But another year slips by
and they remain still to be found.

Transgression

I recall the first erotic dream I had of you
how astonished I was at the transgression of it
and how amazed I was that to you
it appeared so familiar
The delineation of your body was much sharper
than my reveries had ever reasoned
the shadows of your recesses were deeper
unfathomable
Touching each other seemed inessential
your countenance signifying no urgency
Your skin was paler than I imagined
giving off a kind of light
How confused my emotions were on waking
aghast that I may have called out your name
shocked that it should have occurred at all
hungering to go back

You Leave

You get to your feet
you walk to the door – you leave

You do not reach for your bag
shut down your computer
or return to gather pictures of your children

You reach the street
by the stairwell down the hall – you leave

You do not look back
complete your telephone call
or question the different behaviours of others

You walk at a pace
it's the simplest of acts – you leave

You don't look for clues
to make sense of the facts –
you do not need evidence or further affirmation

You don't say goodbyes
The die is cast – you leave

You don't hesitate in the face of change
the time for that is past
Sometimes this is the way you stay alive

Walking

Walking, with no destination
Walking and thinking
Walking and thinking
I will retrace their steps
without deliberation
and rest where they would take a pause

For Henry David Thoreau walked –
As a single footstep
will not make a path on the earth
so a single thought
will not make a pathway in the mind
So we walk, over and over
until our boots scar the land
and we think, over and over
what we need to understand

Walking of a particular kind
I am going walking
I am going walking
Not the distance between door
and somewhere defined
but with a more aimless cause

And Virginia Woolf walked –
When the desire comes upon us
to go street rambling ...
getting up we say:
really, I must buy a pencil
So, excuse your pleasures
with an offhand phrase

to win the time
for these precious days

There's nowhere so lost that you can't get back
and it sharpens your senses
Sharpens your senses
So, walk further
with no fixed tack
to where every breath is yours

Rebecca Solnit walks –
Being out on your own
being free and anonymous
you discover the people around you
So, elect just to walk
and you'll find the reward
where your spirit can sing
and your faith is restored

Choose your own pace
for the pace of your heart
The pace of your heart
Find for yourself
a walkable place
be it forests, lanes or shores

And CS Lewis walked –
The only friend to walk with
is one who so exactly shares your taste
for each mood of the countryside …
But he also said *Don't talk!*
So, choose your company with great care
with no texting, mapping
or soundtrack to disturb the air

Potteric Carr

This spring is no spring
at all; it appears to bring
merely an extension
of winter's slow grind.
A body might get cold
full down to the bone
scraping glints of hope
among the unknown.

We'll laugh and we'll talk
get wrapped up, go walk
down on Potteric Carr
if you feel so inclined.
Our cheeks blooming
from cold wind and sun –
hold each other tightly
till better times come.

Beyond the Salutation

We had not much in common but a love of the outdoors
and to find a way of living with what we'd seen in the wars.
We were of one accord there as we made it through the pass:
we knew no prospect finer than the view up Glen Kirkglass.

Beyond our salutation, there was little need to say
more than *wait a while and see the horses come this way*.
They bring their curiosity, they wear no tack nor brand
but each year when we rest here, the horses are at hand.

Arriving as from nowhere, the dappled and the bay
the chestnut and the piebald; the horses come this way.
I was never one for talking, but we all understand
the power of these moments while the horses are at hand.

I don't recall the circumstance, I don't recall the year –
at the expected time and place my friends did not appear.
There had not been a falling out, the signals maybe crossed
but never did we meet again, all contact then was lost.

Beyond the Salutation is where I made my home
beyond the limits of the town, out by the hippodrome.
I'm wary of the townsfolk now; my counsel is my own –
so rigid in my routine; how small my life has grown.

It seemed there were days when all the world was at my hand
till hard times and misfortune took everything I'd planned.
Of the comforts that I treasure in all that's come to pass
in quiet times I still recall the horses of Kirkglass.

Three Engine Blocks

One was there, concealed in the machair
in the vee of a gully sculpted by an ebullient burn.
It nestled among lumps of jagged Lewisian gneiss
washed now and forever by the dash and deluge;
posing the inevitable question –
occupying the space without ever really belonging.

On the edge of a crag
at the highest point of the moor
among the pink and purple heather
away to one side
as the path twisted at the peak
sat the second;
blackened and dignified,
brutal in the landscape.
A few yards away lay an axle –
wheels still intact – awaiting animation.

At low tide
at the close of the day
number three
revealed itself in the bay.
Radiant, rust-orange,
resplendent on the sand;
harnessed by a frayed
and barnacled band
of rope that led away –
its design revealed –
lashed to a tiny fishing boat
that lay there, keeled.

Woodfield Road

Stepping out with the early paper I just bought
head in the headlines, lost in thought.
Smell of marijuana jangles in my nose
drifting from the window of one of those
big old houses at the top end of Woodfield Road.

Half of me wants to be impressed
by that guy in the jogging bottoms and vest
peering through yellowed nets, clearly off his head.
Don't those people ever need to go to bed
in their rented life on Woodfield Road?

But the other half of me inwardly weeps
that these once-distinguished streets
have broken panes. From this litter-spattered doorway
spew empty cans of Kestrel; there's a burnt-out Cabriolet
down the alleyway off Woodfield Road.

Then, right where the pavement twists,
a paper parcel spills curry, old rice, chips
in a little arc towards the gutter
alongside a cluster of personal clutter –
cosmetics and a sweatshirt soil Woodfield Road.

There are voices that pervade my thoughts –
I'm protective of my locality, feel distraught
at the expectation; at attitudes that sneer:
That's what they're like round here
It's all you expect on Woodfield Road.

Water in the Well

I'll meet you down the marketplace
You should hear all the stories they can tell
I'll meet you down the marketplace

There's water in the well again
It's so long since that crystal water ran
There's water in the well again

They'll ring the village bell again
It's so long since we heard that chiming sound
They'll ring the village bell again

They're dancing in the hall tonight
It's so long since we held each other close
They're dancing in the hall tonight

Then we'll go walking through the fields
Until the morning sun comes over the hill
Then we'll go walking through the fields

The outsiders are coming home
You should hear all the stories they can tell
The outsiders are coming home

When the Waters Rise

You no longer have a choice,
there are soldiers in the street.
The neighbours are stealing food:
they broke down the door in the night.

Water, fire, and light
and a list of things to eat –
serious consideration of weapons,
prospects of fight and flight.

The council offices
burning absurdly in the rain;
disease down in the shopping centre,
gang war in the park,

but we did not make preparations
for all those years in vain:
we will slip out by the alleyway
undercover of the dark.

What do you know of medicine,
can you hunt and fish and cook?
Did you ever skin a rabbit,
did you ever snare a deer?

How will you know the water
is safe to drink down at the brook?
Have you hands to make and mend
a shelter or a spear?

The water's breached the sandbags
it flows beneath the door;
we'll maybe beat it this time
but the game's hardly begun.

The wettest winter this
in two centuries or more –
when the waters rise next time
which way will you run?

Is This What Leaving Feels Like?

Is winter over? It appears to be
dragging its heels
between the then and now
where you and I would have no part to play

And even when I think I am prepared
with plans in place
my best intentions firm
the phone can always catch me unawares –

someone or something I don't want to leave
sowing confusion
fanning the flames against
the forces always pulling us apart

You quickly learn when you live in this town
leaving's a train
that's headed north or south
to somewhere you'll most likely not belong

yet I believe there's someone out there still
who waits for me –
I am convinced of it –
if I can only shake these shackles off

I read somewhere about a palace of mirrors –
one candle flame
illuminates the whole
and lately it's the only dream I have

Renewal

It's now, the needed time for cleansing
and for hoeing of old weeds,
turning of the threadbare soil.

You will be found lacking
if you delay until the Spring.

This is the true time for renewal,
mulching tired memories,
discarding of your failed dreams.

Your chances will be gone
if you bargain for the sun.

Departure

You always had your reasons to remain
close by the sea: not merely the leavings
and arrivings, but your heart's harmony
its own explanation.

By the same token, we were both aware
the time would come when I'd answer the call
of ancient trails, the need to climb and find
a rarer atmosphere.

So, there you stayed once our farewells were done,
beneath the creeping shade of tamarisk;
your books, your water bottle, a few short strides
to reach the water's edge.

Beyond the Espaliered Pear Tree

It was all mine.
In spring, it became a barrier
impenetrable to the eye of the house,
but beyond the pear tree
the air-raid shelter beckoned –
its black mouth,
uneasy smells,
indescribable puddles,
and fears that had to be faced.

And the green shed
that did not seem to be used for anything much –
far too vast for reasonable utility,
but a trove of unnamed rusting machinery,
tins of unidentified treasure,
a gothic mansion of dream and adventure,
with vaulted rafters, sunset bats.

Then, the tree house
hastily assembled by immature hands
in the swaying canopy of a silver birch
using unfamiliar tools.
How did I never fall to earth?

Tom's Territory

Tom was a poacher.
Things were hard for country people;
farm work, when you could get it did not pay a deal.
Tom inherited the tricks –
generations of forebears who took
the products of the country as their right –
to poach was not to steal.

Tom can be found
with his lamp, his snares and flams,
walking stealthily that copse at the top of the rise.
Tom listens to the wind;
there's a good pegger getting up.
Forgoing the pheasant for tonight,
the coneys will be the prize.

Tom watches his step,
and you should too if you should dare
to venture there. Take care not to become the quarry;
Tom might mistake you
for the keeper or the village bobby.
Tread warily in the gloam, my friend
for this is Tom's territory.

Encounter

The first rule, he said, *is there are no rules.*
The second: that there are rules you cannot see.
So walk with me a while and we will speak.

As lives do not follow flawless patterns,
with ebbs and flows to the most undecipherable tides,
and the stories we tell are meandering things
like streams cutting a path through variable terrain,
our conversations do not always begin where they should;
or end.

So, rule number three says find your own road,
while four states:
Whitman, Dickinson, Pound, Rossetti, Elliot,
even Milton,
even the Psalmists set a trail for you to follow.

To answer your question with a question, he said,
How does it start,
this liberation from metric convention?
With a call to the senses?
With random thoughts coalescing around an idea?
With an explosion of emotive force
looking for a form
that can carry its brilliance?

Sometimes freedom is no freedom at all,
so pen your abnormal conventions.
Sometimes freedom is not the right word to use,
so keep the words together that belong together
and be always conscious of what merits being
emphasised.

I thanked him graciously,
but he faded even as my words did.
He had seemed at once so solid
and at the same time a trick of the light.

Crossroads

Who tuned the guitar
that it sings so true,
that it rings so right,
that it burns so bright?
Who tuned the guitar?

Take yourself, some night,
out where highways meet.
Patience, stillness comes,
then a distant note
keening on the wind.

Who was it met you,
led you through graveyards,
Clarksdale to Rosedale?
Out by the Dockery
Plantation you sat,

rested with guitar
cradled on your lap,
listened with longing,
practiced with purpose –
the bargain was struck.

You'll never know peace,
can't ever look back.
Your time won't be long,
but oh, the guitar
it rings out so true.

Termination

At some point there will be an *is that it then?* moment.
But for now, it's a slow withdrawal,
with delays, derailments, and diversions,
procrastinations and protractions.

At some point, affairs will be deemed to be in order;
files will be quite finally filed,
the re-readings re-read and resolved –
accountability absolved.

At some point, the last meeting will be met;
minutes will be signed off,
decisions will be delegated,
roles reappointed or re-allocated.

At some point will be a ceremonial letting go;
a handing over of reins –
the cutting of connections
occasioning equivocal emotions.

At some point there will be an *is that it then?* moment.
But for now, I stare at the walls,
fishing around for the fitting phrase,
yoked by years of yesterdays.

Wide Open

The platform was a lonely place to be;
no one had warned me that my train was lost.
A wind was swirling, and the concrete cold;
I stared along the track to God knows where.
Old certainties were shaken and debased –
I had a world-view that no longer held;
a voice, though willing, searching for its choir.
Wide open to the elements I stood;
I needed something that I couldn't name –
It might be in my pocket, or my dreams.

Thin Skin

How stark is the light that's trained on you
that all the pain in this world
shines so easily through?

Each sentence begins with a stammer
while the tap in the kitchen
drips like a demolition hammer.

The light bulb burns too harshly in this room –
the urgent cry of a grieving heart
striving not to be consumed.

Cruel injustice, you've known more than your share –
there's only so much weight
those bruised shoulders can bear.

So, you reflect on it all with melody and with verse –
your filigree skill in picking
out the beauty in this universe.

How thin is this skin that you are living in;
how choked is this place become
where life relentlessly closes in?

You reach but can't pick up the phone.
Apprehension swarms as you sense
the cold of existence through to the bone.

You will clutch at anything to anchor you fast
so the pieces stop splintering,
mad spinning and drumming be silenced at last.

You ache for the times you can bare your soul –
the relief that you could ever keep
those emotions briefly within your control.

So, you reflect on it all with melody and with verse –
your filigree skill in picking
out all the beauty in this universe.

One Thing More

His fingers kept time on the hospital tray
whose frame cantilevered the width of the bed –
we knew that his breath was slipping away.

His free hand held mine and he asked me to stay;
it went without saying – we left it unsaid.
His fingers kept time on the hospital tray.

His skin somewhat colder, complexion more grey;
the calm in his eyes was tempering my dread –
we knew that his breath was slipping away.

I think of the things it's my duty to say;
words won't form sentences inside my head.
His fingers kept time on the hospital tray.

There is one thing more, his eyes seemed to say
then it's time I faced up to what lies ahead.
We knew that his breath was slipping away.

He reached for the mask, pulled it sharply away:
I'm so proud of all you've achieved, he said.
His fingers kept time on the hospital tray –
we knew that his breath was slipping away.

Past Brodsworth

It starts with a tightening of the throat,
prickling of the skin of my scalp
and the hairs tangibly on end
along the back of my arms and neck.
I am reliving with sensory overload
my Gran tugging at my coat;
pulling me against the wind
along the Roman Ridge.

Before the railways marked the land,
and mines reconstructed our domain,
go back and back as far as you dare
to see what once was there.
Through famine, plague, and flood;
through poverty and plenty,
incursion and invasion –
the slow unfolding of what we are.

This is where it began;
where they paused and observed
the crossing of the river, the lie of the land.
They put down tentative roots,
fashioned shelter and protection,
brought their children, gods, and animals
into this valley
that we now call home.

I must have looked perplexed
but she was patient and persistent:

Look out past Brodsworth towards those moors,
follow the lines of the trees,
the ebb and swell of that ancient terrain;
you will see traces and remains of what made us,
in the light down the valley, the air above the fields
and the prints of your shoes.

Notes and Acknowledgements

Some of these poems appeared in the pamphlets *A Tale to Tell*, published by Glass Head Press in 2017 and *When the Waters Rise*, published by Calder Valley Poetry in 2019.

Thanks are also due to the editors and publishers of the following publications and websites where several of these poems previously appeared: Pennine Platform, Dream Catcher, Dreich, Setu Mag, *The Don and Dearne Collected Poems Vol 1*, Black Bough Poetry's *Christmas & Winter Anthology Vol 1*, and *Christmas & Winter Anthology Vol 2*, the exhibition *these poets, our kin / these poems, our stories* in the Frenchgate Centre Doncaster, The Northern Poetry Library's collaborative online work *Poem of the North*, and the book *Tom's Territory* by Terry Chipp.